Toddler Lesson Plans:
Learning Colors

Ten week guide to help your toddler learn colors

Autumn McKay

CREATIVE IDEAS
PUBLISHING

> Find me on Instagram!
> @BestMomIdeas

Toddler Lesson Plans: Learning Colors by Autumn McKay
Published by Creative Ideas Publishing

www.BestMomIdeas.com

© 2016 Autumn McKay

All rights reserved. No portion of this book may be reproduced in any form without permission from the author, except as permitted by U.S. copyright law.

For permissions contact:
Permissions@BestMomIdeas.com

ISBN: 978-1-952016-07-3

Table of Contents

About Me iv
Introduction v
Unit Overview 1
Red Week Activities 2
Blue Week Activities 4
Yellow Week Activities 6
Green Week Activities 8
White Week Activities 10
Purple Week Activities 12
Brown Week Activities 14
Black Week Activities 16
Orange Week Activities 18
Pink Week Activities 20
Bonus Week 22
Appendix 24
Toddler Lesson Plans: Learning ABC's *Special Preview* 67
Bonus Coloring Pages 79
Thank You Page 83

About Me

My name is Autumn. I am a wife to an incredible husband, and a mother to two precious boys and a sweet little girl! My children are currently 4 years old, 2 years old and 1 year old.

I have a Bachelor of Science degree in Early Childhood Education. I have taught in the classroom and as an online teacher. However, one of my greatest joys is being a mom! After my first son was born in 2013, I wanted to be involved in helping him learn and grow, so I began to develop color lessons to help engage his developing mind. I also wanted to help other moms dealing with hectic schedules and continuous time restraints. As a result, these activities evolved into this book, called *Toddler Lesson Plans: Learning Colors*.

I continued the daily activities with my son, focusing on learning the alphabet and numbers which turned into *Toddler Lesson Plans: Learning ABC's*. Through the last two years I have developed other activities which I have "field tested" with both of my boys. Both of my boys enjoyed these daily activities so much I decided to write another book, called *The Ultimate Toddler Activity Guide*, sharing all the new activities we have done together.

I hope that your little ones can benefit from these color activities just like my boys! I have also developed a website called bestmomideas.com to share other toddler activities, as well as tips and tricks of being a mom that I have learned along the way.

Introduction

Nothing is more charming than a child's face and the many expressions of joy a child exhibits in play. Learning can be so fun! Playtime can be an enjoyable moment for the entire family. Throughout these pages you will find many wonderful activities, which hold the potential to bring a smile to your child's face and joy in your home. My hope is that in the midst of your children "playing their way" to growth and knowledge, this book will help flood your home with joy.

As you begin your journey through this book I need to mention that in most of the activities I address your child with the pronoun "he." I did this for simplicity and ease of writing; however, please know, as I wrote this book I was thinking of your precious little girl as well. I also want to reiterate that the goal of this book is to provide you with activities which you can enjoy with your child. The activities in this book are written for the toddler. However, these years are a time of many developmental milestones. Each child is unique and matures at his or her own pace. If you sense your toddler is becoming frustrated with an activity, please be sensitive and do not push your child to continue. **Without question, you know your child best and what he is capable of attempting.** If you feel an activity is beyond your child's present ability simply move to another activity. There are many great "child tested" activities from which to choose.

Remember, even though significant learning will occur as you engage your child in these color activities, I want you and your child to have fun! Often when my preschooler prays, he ends his prayer with the statement, "…And let us have a fun day, Amen." In the midst of hectic days and the constant pressure to perform, a child deserves a fun day. The truth is you deserve a "fun day" as well. It is my desire that in the following pages you will discover a path for your toddler to learn, and an avenue through which you will experience immense satisfaction as YOU have a fun day and enjoy your child.

Additional Helpful Hints

This book includes activities to help your toddler learn his or her colors. On page 7, an overview of the activities offered each week is provided. There is one activity a day and the activities only take about 10 minutes because a toddler's attention span is very short. Following the Unit Overview is a materials list and step by step instructions for each activity.

I recommend starting these activities around 18 months or later. I did not start these activities with my oldest son until he was almost 21 months old—this was a great age because his communication skills were a little more advanced than they were at 18 months. My second son did not start speaking until he was almost two years old, so I waited to do the activities with him until he was able to speak to avoid frustration for either of us.

Before beginning an activity with your child, simply ask him if he wants to do a fun activity. These activities should not be attempted if your child is resistant to them. You want the learning experience to be enjoyable. Some days, my boys will tell me they do not want to do an activity, and that is totally fine! However, most days both of my sons will ask me if we can do an activity. It makes this mommy's heart happy knowing they want to learn!

I recommend focusing on one color a week, but you are welcome to complete these activities in any order you wish. You can even switch up the order of the colors you want to learn. Seeing the same color over and over each day helps strengthen the connections in your toddler's brain that helps him learn the color. It also helps to review previous colors your toddler has learned.

I know many parents are very busy and do not have a lot of time to set up an activity, so I have placed a "low prep" crayon beside all activities that should only take a minute or two to prepare. I hope these low/no prep activities make life a little easier for you, especially on busy days.

I try to keep an assortment of school supply items in my house to be used for activities so I do not need to constantly shop for supplies. Here is a list of materials used consistently for many of the activities throughout this book if you want to stock up next time you are at the grocery store:

- Construction Paper
- Paper Plates
- Washable Paint
- Paintbrushes
- Index Cards
- Markers
- Pom Poms
- Food Coloring
- Glue (sticks work best for toddlers)
- Fat Crayons
- Scissors (adult and toddler)

I hope these activities bring as much joy and learning to your home as they have mine!

A Gift For You

On appreciation of your purchase of this book, I would like to provide you with a link to the printable appendix pages. This will allow you to have access to appendix pages in color and do your toddler's favorite activity again and again.

www.bestmomideas.com/sendmycolorappendix

Password: bestmomideas9cx1

Unit Overview

	Monday	Tuesday	Wednesday	Thursday	Friday
Red Week	Red Yogurt Finger Paint	🖍 Make an Apple	🖍 Match Red Items	Play in Red Rice	🖍 Red Scavenger Hunt
Blue Week	🖍 Put Blue Pom Poms in Ice Cube Tray	🖍 Put Blueberries in a Basket	🖍 Make Blueberry Muffins	🖍 Paint a Blue Bird	🖍 Blue Scavenger Hunt
Yellow Week	Yellow Balloon Bath	🖍 Paint a Sun	Stack Yellow Rings	🖍 Make Yellow Playdough	🖍 Yellow Scavenger Hunt
Green Week	🖍 Color a Frog	Green Food Taste Test	🖍 Play Red Light, Green Light	Scoop Green Water	🖍 Green Scavenger Hunt
White Week	🖍 Play in Shaving Cream	🖍 Sticker Name	🖍 Make a Sheep	Snowball Bowling	🖍 White Scavenger Hunt
Purple Week	🖍 Make Grapes	🖍 Make a Purple Cow Float	String Purple Fruit Loops	🖍 Purple Line Tracing	🖍 Purple Scavenger Hunt
Brown Week	🖍 Color a Bear	Make a Dirt Sundae	Owl Puzzle	Match Brown Shapes	🖍 Brown Scavenger Hunt
Black Week	🖍 Paint a Spider	Name Animal Shadows	🖍 Black Bean Sensory Bin	Zebra Marble Painting	🖍 Black Scavenger Hunt
Orange Week	🖍 Paint a Pumpkin	🖍 Make Pumpkin Muffins	🖍 Paint a Carrot with Carrots	🖍 Goldfish Counting	🖍 Orange Scavenger Hunt
Pink Week	Pink Bubble Bin	🖍 Color a Flamingo	Corral the Pigs	🖍 Make Pink Cookies*	🖍 Pink Scavenger Hunt
Bonus Week	Sort Pom Poms	Color Hop	Easter Egg Matching	Ice Cube Painting	Pin the Tail on the Bunny

RED ACTIVITY WEEK

MONDAY

Red Yogurt Finger Paint

Materials
- ☐ 6oz Carton of Plain or Vanilla Yogurt
- ☐ Red Kool-Aid Packet or Red Food Coloring

Directions

Ask your toddler if he would enjoy painting in yogurt. Mix together the yogurt and the whole packet of Kool-Aid with a spoon. Place your toddler at the table or in a high chair and let him paint with the red yogurt. I poured all of the yogurt mixture on my son's high chair tray since he was being timid with it at first. This encouraged him to get messy and really play in it! As your toddler is playing, tell him the color of the paint; and ask him to tell you the color of the paint. Show him how to draw numbers, shapes, and letters with your finger in the yogurt paint while it is spread out on the surface.

My sons enjoyed this activity so much that we did it each week with the new color we were learning.

TUESDAY

Make an Apple

Materials
- ☐ Apple Activity Page (Appendix A)
- ☐ Red Construction Paper
- ☐ Glue Stick

Directions

Show your toddler the red construction paper. Tell him the paper is red. Ask him to repeat the word "red" to you. Now show your toddler how to tear the red construction paper. Help him tear the red paper into many pieces; the pieces can be any size or shape. When he has finished tearing the red paper, show him how to use the glue stick to rub glue on the *Apple* activity page. This activity was the first time my son used glue, so I let him try it a couple of times and then I spread the glue all over the apple for him. Once the glue is on the *Apple* activity page, have your toddler place his red paper all over the apple. As you are completing this activity, tell your toddler what color the apple is, and ask him to tell you the color of the apple. After allowing an appropriate time for the glue to dry, be sure to hang the picture in a special place, like the refrigerator, so he knows you are proud of his work.

RED ACTIVITY WEEK

WEDNESDAY

✏️ Match Red Items

Materials
- ☐ Red Pictures Activity Page (Appendix B)
- ☐ Scissors

Directions

You will need to cut out the red pictures provided on the *Red Pictures* activity page. Ask your toddler to sit beside you. Lay the pictures out next to each other so your toddler can see there are two of each picture. Let him identify the object in each picture. Ask him the color of each picture. With each matched set of pictures, remove one of the pictures. There should now be one set of pictures in front of your toddler, with the corresponding matching pictures in your hand. Give your toddler one of the red pictures you have in your hand, and ask him to place it next to its match.

If your toddler needs a challenge, mix up all of the red pictures and ask him to collect the matches.

THURSDAY

Play in Red Rice

Materials
- ☐ 5 Cups of Rice
- ☐ 2 ½ Teaspoons of Vinegar
- ☐ Red Food Coloring
- ☐ Cookie Sheet or Wax Paper
- ☐ Plastic Container with Lid
- ☐ Bowl
- ☐ Shovels, Scoops, Cups, etc.

Directions

Please note: the dyed rice used in this activity should be dried for 24 hours before it is used in an activity with your child. To dye the rice, pour five cups of rice into a small plastic container and add 2 ½ teaspoons of vinegar and 6 to 7 drops of red food coloring (the more food coloring you add the redder the rice). Put the lid on the container, and shake it until all the rice is red. Once your rice is evenly coated, spread it out in an even layer on a cookie sheet or wax paper, and allow it to dry for 24 hours.

When the rice is dry, pour it into a bowl. Your child will love scooping it, shoveling it, or pouring it into other containers. You can also hide various items in the red rice and allow your child the thrill of digging for buried treasure. As your toddler is having fun playing in the rice ask him the color of the rice.

FRIDAY

✏️ Red Scavenger Hunt

Materials
- ☐ Bag or Bucket
- ☐ Red items

Directions

Since you have taught your child the color red this week, it's now time to see if your child can identify red items around the house. Give your little one a bag or bucket (we used our trick or treat bucket) and tell him you are going on a scavenger hunt around the house to look for the color red. When he finds a red object, he can place it in his bucket. You might need to guide him to a few red items to help him understand how to do the activity. My son found red items such as Legos, balls, an apple, and toy cars.

BLUE ACTIVITY WEEK

MONDAY

Put Blue Pom Poms in an Ice Cube Tray

Materials
- ☐ Blue Pom Poms
- ☐ Small Tongs
- ☐ Ice Cube Tray

Directions

Show your toddler the blue pom poms, and tell him the pom poms are blue. Show your toddler how to pick up the blue pom poms with the tongs and place the blue pom poms in the ice cube tray. Let your little one try. This activity will help him work on his hand-eye coordination and fine motor skills. As your toddler is placing the blue pom poms in the ice cube tray ask him to tell you the color of the pom poms.

You can also introduce counting to your toddler by asking him to place one pom pom in an ice cube compartment, two in the next, and so on.

TUESDAY

Put Blueberries in a Basket

Materials
- ☐ Blueberry Basket Activity Page (Appendix C)
- ☐ Blueberries, Blue Pom Poms, Blue M&M's

Directions

Ask your toddler if he would enjoy counting blueberries. Show him the *Blueberry Basket* activity page. Show him that each basket of blueberries has a number on the basket. Point to the numbers as you say the number out loud to your toddler. Ask him to say the numbers with you. Now place a bowl of blueberries, blue pom poms or blue M&M's, in front of your toddler. Ask him the color of the blueberries (pom poms, or M&M's). Explain to him that he will place the same amount of blueberries on the basket as the number written on the basket.

For example, point to the number one. Tell him it is the number one, so he will place one blueberry on the basket. If this is the first time you are introducing numbers to your toddler, give him one blueberry at a time to place on the basket. Before moving to the next basket, point to each blueberry and count them out loud. As you count the blueberries, ask your toddler to count out loud with you, or to say the number after you say it.

Toddler Lesson Plans: Learning Colors | Autumn McKay

BLUE ACTIVITY WEEK

WEDNESDAY

Make Blueberry Muffins

Materials
- ☐ Package of Blueberry Muffin Mix
- ☐ Ingredients on the Package
- ☐ Bowl
- ☐ Spoon
- ☐ Muffin Pan
- ☐ Cooking Spray

Directions

For ease in preparation, I bought a box of blueberry muffin mix instead of making homemade blueberry muffins. I poured real blueberries into the mix so my son could see the blueberries. I applaud you if you choose to make homemade blueberry muffins!

Let your toddler help pour the ingredients into the bowl and mix them together. I sprayed the muffin pan with cooking spray, but my son poured the ingredients into the bowl and stirred it together, and with some assistance scooped the mixture into the muffin pan. Explain to your toddler that blueberries are blue. Ask him what color the blueberries are as well. Enjoy eating the muffins together!

THURSDAY

Paint a Blue Bird

Materials
- ☐ Bird Activity Page (Appendix D)
- ☐ Blue Paint
- ☐ Paper Plate
- ☐ Paintbrush
- ☐ Clothes Pin
- ☐ Cotton Ball

Directions

Show your toddler the *Bird* activity page. Explain to him that he will paint the bird the color blue. Squirt some blue paint on a paper plate. Explain to your toddler that paint only goes on paper. You can let your toddler use a paintbrush to paint the bird.

Since my son was young at the time of these activities, I found that he had better control of a homemade paintbrush I made. I placed a cotton ball in a clothes pin. As your toddler is painting, ask him what color he is painting the bird. When your toddler's picture has finished drying, display his work in a special place so he can be proud of his work.

FRIDAY

Blue Scavenger Hunt

Materials
- ☐ Bag or Bucket
- ☐ Blue items

Directions

Since you have been teaching your child about the color blue all week, it's now time to see if your child can find blue items around the house. Give your little one a bag or bucket and tell him you are going on a scavenger hunt around the house to look for the color blue. When he finds a blue item, he can place it in his bucket. My son was able to find items such as his blue bird, his cup, a ball, and a crayon.

YELLOW ACTIVITY WEEK

MONDAY

Yellow Balloon Bath

Materials
- ☐ Yellow Balloons
- ☐ Bathtub

Directions

Fill up eight yellow balloons with water. Place the balloons in the bathtub. Fill the bathtub with water to the level you use for your child's bath. Let your toddler take a bath with the yellow balloons. Tell him the balloons are yellow, and ask him what color the balloons are as he continues to play.

If it is warm outside, you and your little one can play with the yellow water balloons outside too!

TUESDAY

✎ Paint a Sun

Materials
- ☐ Sun Activity Page (Appendix E)
- ☐ Yellow Paint
- ☐ Paper Plate
- ☐ Paintbrush

Directions

You will need the *Sun* activity page. Show the sun to your toddler, and tell him the sun is yellow and he is going to paint the sun yellow. Squirt some yellow paint on a paper plate. Give your toddler a paintbrush, and let him paint his sun. You can also use the "homemade paintbrush" I mentioned in the *Paint a Blue Bird* activity. We have also discovered that Do-A-Dot markers are a lot of fun to use.

As your toddler is painting ask him what color he is painting the sun. When your toddler's picture is finished drying, find a special place to hang the sun picture.

Yellow Activity Week

WEDNESDAY

✏️ Stack Yellow Rings

Materials
- ☐ Yellow Paint
- ☐ Paintbrush
- ☐ 3 Toilet Paper Tubes
- ☐ Standing Paper Towel Holder
- ☐ Scissors

Directions

Paint the outside of three toilet paper tubes yellow, and let them dry. Once they are dry, cut them into fourths, creating four "rings." Please note: To ensure the paint on the rings has dried properly, it is best to paint the tubes the day before this activity is attempted.

Once your rings are ready, ask your toddler if he would like to stack the rings. Place the paper towel holder in front of your toddler and ask him to slide the rings over the paper towel holder. Ask your toddler what color the rings are as he stacks them. You can also count the rings together as he stacks them.

THURSDAY

✏️ Make Yellow Playdough

Materials
- ☐ 1 ½ Cups of Flour
- ☐ ½ Cup of Salt
- ☐ 2 Teaspoons of Cream of Tartar
- ☐ 2 Tablespoons of Oil
- ☐ 1 Cup of Boiling Water
- ☐ Yellow Food Coloring
- ☐ Playdough Toys

Directions

Ask your toddler if he would like to help you make playdough. Ask your toddler to help you mix the flour, salt, cream of tartar, oil, water, and food coloring together in a large bowl. Remind your little one that the water is very hot, so only mommy can touch the water. The mixture will be a little clumpy as you mix it together, so knead it a few times to smooth it out. If it is too sticky, you can add more flour. If the mixture is too clumpy, add more boiling water.

Once your playdough is ready, your toddler can play in it. Let your little one use some playdough toys to shape it, roll it, or cut it. Cookie cutters are also a fun tool to use when playing with playdough. As your child is playing with the playdough ask him the color of the playdough.

FRIDAY

✏️ Yellow Scavenger Hunt

Materials
- ☐ Bag or Bucket
- ☐ Yellow Items

Directions

Ask your toddler if he would like to go on a scavenger hunt to find different yellow objects around the house. Give your little one a bag or bucket, and ask him if he can find something yellow to place in his bag. You can direct him towards something yellow if he needs help. When he finds the yellow items, he can place it in his bag. Examples of the yellow items we found are: a banana, a toy car, and the handle on a play tool.

GREEN ACTIVITY WEEK

MONDAY

Color a Frog

Materials
- ☐ Frog Activity Page (Appendix F)
- ☐ Fat Green Crayon

Directions

Show your toddler the picture of the *Frog* activity page. Ask your toddler what is on the activity page. Explain to him that frogs are green, and he will color the frog green. The fat crayon will be much easier for your toddler to hold and manipulate. As your little one is coloring ask him what color he is coloring the frog. When your toddler is finished coloring; hang the picture somewhere that he can be proud of his work.

TUESDAY

Green Food Taste Test

Materials
- ☐ Muffin Pan
- ☐ Green Food (Ex. Celery, Green Grapes, Kiwi, Cucumbers, Peppers, Broccoli, etc.)

Directions

Prepare the activity by slicing up samples of an assortment of green foods. You can use foods such as: broccoli, kiwi, green apples, green grapes, celery, cucumbers, peppers, and green M&M's. Place one green food item in each muffin pan cup.

Ask your toddler if he would enjoy tasting different kinds of green food. Show him the muffin pan full of green food. Ask your child to tell you the color of the food in the muffin pan. Ask him which food he would like to try first. After he eats it, ask him if he liked the food item. Do this for each sample he tastes.

GREEN **ACTIVITY WEEK**

WEDNESDAY

Play Red Light, Green Light

Materials
- ☐ Red Construction Paper
- ☐ Green Construction Paper
- ☐ Lots of Room to Run

Directions

Ask your toddler if he would like to play a fun running game. Explain to your toddler that when you hold up a green piece of paper and say, "Green Light," that means he can run fast towards you. Tell him when you hold up a red piece of paper and say, "Red Light," he needs to stop and freeze. Show him the pieces of paper as you explain the rules. I explained the rules to my sons a couple of times, and asked them to tell me the rules. I repeated this until I knew they understood the rules of our game.

Once you explain the rules, you can play the game outside or inside. Have your toddler stand on one side of the yard as you stand on the other side. Hold up the green paper and say, "Green Light." Let your toddler begin to run to you. Now switch to the red paper and say, "Red Light." Tell your toddler to freeze. Continue to do this until he makes it to you. This activity will help enhance your toddler's listening skills.

THURSDAY

Scoop Green Water

Materials
- ☐ Muffin Pan
- ☐ Green Food Coloring
- ☐ Big Bowl
- ☐ Scoops, Spoons, and Measuring Cups

Directions

This activity is a good outside activity, but if it's too cold outside the bathtub works well too. Ask your toddler if he would like to play in green water. Fill a big bowl full of water. Use the green food coloring to dye the water green.

Place the bowl of green water in front of your toddler. Ask him the color of the water. Now give your toddler an empty muffin pan, spoons, scoops, or measuring cups. Let him fill the muffin pan with the green water. As he is playing with the green water, ask him to tell you the color of the water.

FRIDAY

Green Scavenger Hunt

Materials
- ☐ Bag or Bucket
- ☐ Green Items

Directions

Since you have been teaching your child about the color green this week, it is now time to see if your child can identify green items around the house. Ask your toddler if he is ready to go on a scavenger hunt to look for green objects. Give your little one a bag or bucket. Ask him to find some objects that are green to place in his bag. If it is spring or summer time, you can take your little one outside to find green items in nature as well. Several green items we discovered: grass, leaves, balls and a tractor.

Toddler Lesson Plans: Learning Colors | Autumn McKay

WHITE ACTIVITY WEEK

MONDAY

Play in Shaving Cream

Materials
☐ Shaving Cream

Directions
Explain to your toddler he will be learning about the color white this week. Tell him he will get to play in shaving cream. Place your toddler in his high chair or at the table and spray some shaving cream in front of him. Point to the shaving cream and tell him it is white. Let him squish the shaving cream between his fingers, move it around, and draw in it. As he is playing ask him the color of the shaving cream.

TUESDAY

Sticker Name

Materials
☐ Construction Paper
☐ Marker
☐ White Hole Reinforcement Stickers

Directions
You will need to write your child's name on a piece of construction paper using a marker. Write your child's name in all capital letters. As a child is learning to recognize letters it is easier for him to start this process by learning capital letters.

Ask your toddler if he would like to write his name with white stickers. Show him the piece of paper with his name on it. Point to each letter as you say it, and then swipe your finger under his name as you read his name. Explain to your toddler that you will hand him a white sticker and he will place the sticker along the lines of each letter. You may need to show your child how to place the sticker along the lines. As he is placing his stickers on his name ask him the color of the stickers.

Toddler Lesson Plans: Learning Colors | Autumn McKay

WHITE ACTIVITY WEEK

WEDNESDAY

Make a Sheep

Materials
- ☐ Sheep Activity Page (Appendix G)
- ☐ Cotton Balls
- ☐ Glue stick

Directions

Ask your toddler if he would enjoy making a fluffy, white sheep. Show him the *Sheep* activity page. Explain to your toddler you are going to make the sheep have fluffy, white wool by gluing cotton balls on the sheep. Show your toddler how to use the glue stick to spread glue all over the sheep's body. You may need to assist him but allow him to try to spread the glue on the picture himself. Once the sheep's body is covered in glue your toddler can start placing cotton balls on the sheep. I split the cotton balls in half so they would stick to the glue better. As you are working with your toddler ask him the color of the sheep. When your toddler is finished placing the cotton balls on his sheep pick a special place to hang the picture with your toddler.

THURSDAY

Snowball Bowling

Materials
- ☐ 3 Balled Up Socks
- ☐ 6 Solo Cups

Directions

Ask your toddler if he would like to go bowling with white snowballs. You will need to ball up three pairs of socks to look like snowballs. Show your toddler the snowballs, and ask him to tell you their color. Now stack six Solo cups in a pyramid formation with three on the bottom, two in the middle, and one on the top. Ask your toddler to stand about five feet away from the cups. Explain to him that he will roll the white snowballs, one at a time, towards the cups to try to knock them down. Tell him he gets three attempts to knock all of the cups down. This is a fun game that we played many times!

FRIDAY

White Scavenger Hunt

Materials
- ☐ Bag or Bucket
- ☐ White Items

Directions

Since your child has been learning about white all week, it's now time to see if your child can find white objects around your home. Give your little one a bag or bucket and tell him that he is going on a scavenger hunt around the house to look for things that are white. When he finds the white items, he can place the white objects in his bucket. You can guide him to a few white items to help him understand the objective of the activity. Examples of the white items we found: socks, a piece of paper, stuffed animal, and diapers.

PURPLE ACTIVITY WEEK

MONDAY

✏ Make Grapes

Materials
- ☐ Grapes Activity Page (Appendix H)
- ☐ Purple Construction Paper
- ☐ Glue Stick

Directions

Show your toddler the *Grapes* activity page. Tell him that grapes can be purple, so he will use purple paper to make the grapes purple. Show your toddler how to tear the purple construction paper. Help him tear the purple paper into many pieces; they can be any size or shape. Now show your toddler how to use the glue stick to spread glue on the *Grapes* activity page. Let him try to spread glue on the activity page by himself. Once the glue is on the *Grapes* activity page, have him place his purple paper all over the grapes. As you are completing this activity, tell your toddler what color the grapes are and ask him for the color of the grapes. When your toddler completes his grapes ask him where he would like to hang his picture.

TUESDAY

✏ Make a Purple Cow Float

Materials
- ☐ Vanilla Ice Cream
- ☐ Grape Juice
- ☐ Bowl
- ☐ Spoon

Directions

Ask your toddler if he would enjoy making a fun purple snack called a purple cow float. This is just like a root beer float you might have had as a child. Scoop some vanilla ice cream into a bowl. Next, let your little one help you pour a little bit of grape juice over the ice cream. You can also add some lemon-lime soda to the bowl. We just did grape juice since we choose not to drink soda. Let your toddler enjoy his tasty snack. Ask your toddler what color his snack is as he is eating.

Purple Activity Week

WEDNESDAY

String Purple Fruit Loops

Materials
- ☐ String or Pipe Cleaner
- ☐ Purple Fruit Loops

Directions

Make a big pile of purple fruit loops for your toddler Ask your toddler the color of the fruit loops. Explain to your toddler that he will place the string or pipe cleaner through the hole in the fruit loop. We used a pipe cleaner because it was sturdier than string, but you can use string too. As he is stringing the fruit loops on the pipe cleaner ask him the color of the fruit loops. When he is finished, you can make it into a bracelet or necklace. He can snack on his creation throughout the day.

THURSDAY

Purple Line Tracing

Materials
- ☐ Purple Line Tracing Activity Page (Appendix I)
- ☐ Fat Purple Crayon

Directions

Show your toddler the *Purple Line Tracing* activity page. Ask him the color of the lines. Let him trace the lines with his finger. Tell him that he will use a purple crayon to trace the lines. Now give your child a purple crayon and show him how to hold it properly. Let him try tracing the lines himself. If your toddler needs assistance tracing you may guide his hand.

FRIDAY

Purple Scavenger Hunt

Materials
- ☐ Bag or Bucket
- ☐ Purple Items

Directions

Ask your toddler if he would like to go for a purple scavenger hunt. Give your little one a bag or bucket and tell him he is going on a scavenger hunt around the house to look for objects that are the color purple. When he finds a purple object, he can put it in his bucket. Examples of the purple items we found: magnets, grapes, a book, and balls.

BROWN ACTIVITY WEEK

MONDAY

✏️ Color a Bear

Materials
- ☐ Bear Activity Page (Appendix J)
- ☐ Fat Brown Crayon

Directions
Ask your toddler if he would like to color a picture of a bear. Tell him that he will be learning about the color brown this week, so he will color the bear brown. As your little one is coloring, ask him the color of the bear. When your toddler is finished coloring his bear ask him to find a special place he would like to hang his picture.

TUESDAY

Make a Dirt Sundae

Materials (FOR 2 SERVINGS)
- ☐ Chocolate Pudding (2 snack packs or 1 small box)
- ☐ 8 Oreos
- ☐ 4 Gummy Worms
- ☐ 2 Clear Cups

Directions
Ask your toddler to assist you in preparing the chocolate pudding ahead of time. While the pudding is firming in the refrigerator let your toddler help you smash the Oreos. I like to put the Oreos in a Ziploc bag, and let my son stomp on them with his feet, but be careful because the bag can open.

Once the Oreos are smashed, you are ready to assemble your dirt sundae. Pour a layer of cookie crumbs in the bottom of the cup—covering the bottom. Top with a layer of pudding. Next, top the pudding with another layer of cookie crumbs. Top with another layer of chocolate pudding. Now add two gummy worms to each cup. As you are preparing the snack with your toddler ask him to tell you the color of the pudding. Enjoy your tasty treat!

Brown Activity Week

Wednesday

Owl Puzzle

Materials
- ☐ Owl Puzzle Activity Page (Appendix K)
- ☐ Scissors

Directions

Ask your toddler if he would enjoy putting an owl puzzle together. Show him the *Owl Puzzle* activity page. Ask your toddler the color of the owl. Explain that you will cut the owl out, and then he will need to put the owl back together. Cut the owl puzzle out along the strips. Mix up the pieces and place the pieces in front of your toddler. Ask him to put the owl back together. Praise your little one when he completes the puzzle!

Thursday

Match Brown Shapes

Materials
- ☐ Brown Shape Activity Pages (Appendix L)
- ☐ Scissors

Directions

Show your toddler the *Brown Shape* activity pages. Ask him the color of the shapes. Now point to each shape and ask your toddler if he can tell you the name of the shape. If this is the first time he is being introduced to shapes, point to each shape and tell him the name of the shape. Ask him to repeat the name back to you.

Explain to your toddler you will cut the brown shapes out, and he will need to match the brown shape to the correct shape outline on the paper. Praise him when he matches the shape correctly.

Friday

Brown Scavenger Hunt

Materials
- ☐ Bag or Bucket
- ☐ Brown Items

Directions

Since your child has been learning about the color brown all week, ask your toddler if he would enjoy finding brown objects to place in his bag. You can do this scavenger hunt inside or outside. Give your little one a bag or bucket, and tell him he is going on a scavenger hunt to look for the color brown. When he finds something brown he can put it in his bag. We chose to do this scavenger hunt outside. Examples of the brown colored items we found: mulch, tree bark, leaves, and rocks.

BLACK ACTIVITY WEEK

MONDAY

✏ Paint a Spider

Materials
- ☐ Spider Activity Page (Appendix M)
- ☐ Black Paint
- ☐ Paper Plate
- ☐ Paintbrush

Directions

Show your toddler the *Spider* activity page. Tell him that he will learn about the color black this week, so he will be painting the spider black. Squirt some black paint on a paper plate. Give your toddler a paintbrush to use to paint his spider.

You can also let your toddler paint his spider using his fingers or a sponge. It is fun to experiment with different methods of painting. As your toddler is painting ask him what color he is painting the spider. When your toddler's painting is finished drying, find a special place to hang his artwork.

TUESDAY

Name Animal Shadows

Materials
- ☐ Animal Shadow Activity Page (Appendix N)
- ☐ Scissors

Directions

Ask your toddler if he would enjoy identifying animals from looking at their shadows. Cut out the animal shadow cards from the *Animal Shadow* activity page. Show your toddler a card with a shadow on it. Ask him the color of the shadow on the card. Now ask him if he can name what type of animal is on the card by looking at its shadow. Do this for each animal shadow.

BLACK ACTIVITY WEEK

WEDNESDAY

Black Bean Sensory Bin

Materials
- ☐ Bag of Black Beans
- ☐ Shovels, Measuring Cups, Scoops
- ☐ Plastic Container
- ☐ Small Black Toys (optional)

Directions

You will need to pour a large bag of black beans into a plastic container or bowl. If you have small black toys, hide a few of those items in the black beans. Now let your toddler hunt for the black toys.

You can also let your toddler scoop and transfer the black beans from one bowl to another bowl. This is just as fun! As your little one is playing, ask him the color of the beans.

THURSDAY

Zebra Marble Painting

Materials
- ☐ Zebra Activity Page (Appendix O)
- ☐ Black Paint
- ☐ Marble
- ☐ Tape
- ☐ Box

Directions

You will need to cut out the picture of the zebra from the *Zebra* activity page. Show the zebra to your toddler, and explain that the zebra has lost all of his black stripes. Ask your toddler if he would like to help put the black stripes back on the zebra by using a marble.

Tape the zebra to the bottom of a box. A shoe box or gift box is a good size box to use. Now dip a marble in black paint. Place the marble on the zebra in the box. Ask your toddler to move the box around so that the marble begins to roll and make stripes on the zebra. You can dip the marble in the black paint multiple times if needed. When your toddler is finished, ask him what color stripes he painted on the zebra. Let the zebra dry, and then you and your toddler can find a special place to hang the happy zebra.

FRIDAY

Black Scavenger Hunt

Materials
- ☐ Bag or Bucket
- ☐ Black Items

Directions

Ask your toddler if he would enjoy hunting for black toys around the house. Give him a bag or bucket and tell him as soon as he spies a black toy or object to race over to it and place it in his bag. You can help guide him by telling him if he is hot or cold as he searches. If he is really close to a black object, tell him he is hot. If he is far away from a black object tell him he is cold. Examples of the black colored items we found are: a remote control, toy cars, beans, and crayons.

MONDAY

Paint a Pumpkin

Materials

- ☐ Pumpkin Activity Page (Appendix P)
- ☐ Orange Paint
- ☐ Paper Plate
- ☐ Paintbrush

Directions

Show your toddler the *Pumpkin* activity page. Tell your toddler that pumpkins are orange. Ask him to say the word "orange" with you. Tell him that he will paint the pumpkin orange. Squirt some orange paint on a paper plate, and give a paintbrush to your toddler. Ask him to paint his pumpkin. As he is painting his pumpkin, ask him what color he is using to paint the pumpkin. When he is finished painting, let his pumpkin painting dry, and then let your toddler pick a place to hang his picture.

TUESDAY

Make Pumpkin Muffins

Materials

- ☐ Muffin Pan
- ☐ Cooking Spray
- ☐ 1 15 Ounce Can of Pumpkin Puree
- ☐ 4 Eggs
- ☐ 1 Cup of Vegetable Oil
- ☐ 2/3 Cups of Water
- ☐ 3 Cups of Sugar
- ☐ 3 ½ Cups of All-Purpose Flour
- ☐ 2 Teaspoons of Baking Soda
- ☐ 1 ½ Teaspoon of Salt
- ☐ 1 Teaspoon of Cinnamon
- ☐ 1 Teaspoon of Ground Nutmeg
- ☐ ½ Teaspoon of Ground Cloves
- ☐ ¼ Teaspoon of Ginger

Directions

Ask your toddler if he would enjoy helping you make pumpkin muffins. To make the muffins, you will need to grease your muffin pan. Now let your toddler help you pour the following ingredients into a mixing bowl: the pumpkin puree, eggs, oil, water, and sugar. Ask your toddler the color of the pumpkin puree. Mix the ingredients in your bowl until well blended.

In a separate bowl, let your toddler help you whisk the remaining ingredients together. Combine the dry ingredients and the pumpkin mixture. Stir until blended.

Now scoop the mixture into the muffin pan. Bake at 350 degrees Fahrenheit for about 22-27 minutes. When the timer runs out insert a toothpick in the center of a muffin—if it comes out clean, the muffins are done; but if the batter comes out on the toothpick, the muffins need to cook longer. Let the muffins cool for a few minutes. Afterwards, you and your toddler can enjoy a nice snack!

ORANGE ACTIVITY WEEK

WEDNESDAY

Paint a Carrot with Carrots

Materials
- ☐ Carrot Activity Page (Appendix Q)
- ☐ Carrots
- ☐ Orange Paint
- ☐ Paper Plate

Directions

Show your toddler the *Carrot* activity page. Ask him the color of the carrot. Ask your toddler if he would like to paint the picture of a carrot orange using carrots as a paintbrush. I cut a whole carrot in half for my son to use like a stamp to paint his carrot. When the carrot painting is dry, you can help your toddler find a spot on the refrigerator to hang his masterpiece.

THURSDAY

Goldfish Counting

Materials
- ☐ Goldfish Crackers
- ☐ Index Cards
- ☐ Marker

Directions

Write the numbers 1-5 on index cards. There should be one number on each index card. Place the index cards in order in front of your toddler. Ask him to help you count. Point to each number as you say it; wait for your toddler to say the number before saying the next number. Tell your toddler that he will get to count with goldfish today. Place a bowl of goldfish next to him. Ask him the color of the goldfish. Now point to the number one, ask him what number it is, and then ask him how many goldfish he needs to place on the card. Do this for each index card.

If your toddler needs to be challenged, then you can write numbers 1-10 on the index cards for your toddler to count.

FRIDAY

Orange Scavenger Hunt

Materials
- ☐ Bag or Bucket
- ☐ Orange Items

Directions

Ask your toddler if he would enjoy going on an orange scavenger hunt. Give your little one a bag or bucket, and explain to him he will need to find things that are the color orange to place in his bag. When he finds an orange object, he can place it in his bag. You can show him an example of an orange object to place in his bag. Examples of the orange colored items we found are: an orange, a basketball, and books.

Toddler Lesson Plans: Learning Colors | Autumn McKay

PINK ACTIVITY WEEK

MONDAY

Pink Bubble Bin

Materials
- ☐ Dish Soap
- ☐ Whisks
- ☐ Large Plastic Container
- ☐ Water
- ☐ Pink or Red Food Coloring
- ☐ Cups

Directions

Ask your toddler if he would like to play in a bucket of pink bubbles. Fill the plastic container with water and add some dish soap. Add some pink food coloring. If you don't have pink food coloring, you can do a few drops of red food coloring. Let your toddler whisk it together until the bubbles start to turn pink. Ask your toddler the color of the bubbles. Let him play in the pink bubbles with the whisk, cups, or his hands. As your toddler is playing, tell him what color the bubbles are, and be sure to ask him the color of the bubbles as well.

TUESDAY

Color a Flamingo

Materials
- ☐ Flamingo Activity Page (Appendix R)
- ☐ Pink Crayon

Directions

Show your toddler the *Flamingo* activity page. Tell him it is a picture of a flamingo. Tell him flamingos are pink, so he will use a pink crayon to color the flamingo pink. As your little one is coloring, ask him the color of the flamingo. When he finishes coloring his picture find a special place to hang is art work.

PINK ACTIVITY WEEK

WEDNESDAY

Corral the Pigs

Materials
- ☐ 10 Pink Balloons
- ☐ Fly Swatter

Directions
This is a fun activity to do outside, but it can also be done inside. You will need to blow up 10 pink balloons. Place the balloons in the yard or around the house. Explain to your toddler that the gate was left open to the pig pen and all of the pink pigs got out of the pig pen. Tell him that he will need to use the fly swatter to gather up all of the pigs into one corner of the yard. Encourage him as he is playing, and congratulate him when he completes the activity.

THURSDAY

Make Pink Cookies

Materials
- ☐ 1 Box of Strawberry Cake Mix
- ☐ 1 Teaspoon Baking Powder
- ☐ 2 Eggs
- ☐ ⅓ Cup of Vegetable Oil
- ☐ ½ Teaspoon of Vanilla Extract
- ☐ 1 ¼ Cups of Semi-sweet Chocolate Chips
- ☐ Cooking Spray
- ☐ Cookie Sheet
- ☐ Mixing Bowl
- ☐ Wire Rack
- ☐ Spoon

Directions
Ask your toddler if he would enjoy making pink cookies. Preheat the oven to 350 degrees Fahrenheit. Spray your cookie sheet with cooking spray.

In a large bowl, ask your toddler to pour in the cake mix and baking powder. Mix together and set aside.

In a smaller bowl, ask your toddler to help you whisk together the eggs, oil, and vanilla by hand. Now add the egg mixture to the cake mixture, and stir to form dough—be sure there are no cake mix clumps. Ask your toddler to gently fold in the chocolate chips.

Now you are ready to drop rounded balls of dough, about two tablespoons each, onto the cookie sheet. Bake for 10 minutes.

When the cookies are finished baking, let them cool on the cookie sheet for about three minutes before transferring to a wire rack to cool completely. As you and your toddler are baking, ask him to tell you the color of the cookies you are making. Enjoy your tasty treat!

FRIDAY

Pink Scavenger Hunt

Materials
- ☐ Bag or Bucket
- ☐ Pink Items

Directions
Ask your little one if he would like to go on a fun scavenger hunt to find pink items around the house. Give your little one a bag or bucket and tell him he is going to find different pink objects and place them in his bag. You can help guide him to a pink object to show him an example of what he needs to do. Examples of the pink items we found are: mommy's shirt, strawberry applesauce, our cookies, and blocks.

MONDAY

Sort Pom Poms

Materials
- ☐ Assortment of Pom Poms
- ☐ Muffin Pan
- ☐ Construction Paper
- ☐ Scissors

Directions

Using the various colors of construction paper, cut out a red, blue, yellow, green, white, orange, pink, purple, brown, and black circle. The circle needs to fit into the bottom of muffin pan cup. Place a circle in each muffin pan cup.

Ask your toddler if he would like to match pom poms to the correct colored circle. Place an assortment of pom poms in front of your toddler. Let him pick up a pom pom. Ask him what color the pom pom is, and then ask him to place it in the matching colored muffin pan cup. To help develop your toddler's fine motor skills you can allow him to use tongs to sort the pom poms. When your little one has completed the activity ask him if he would like to count how many pom poms of each color are in the muffin pan cups.

BONUS **WEEK ACTIVITIES**

TUESDAY

Color Hop

Materials
- ☐ Chalk

Directions

Ask your toddler if he would enjoy doing an activity outside. Outside on the driveway, or on another appropriate surface, use colored chalk and draw some shapes in the different colors you and your toddler have learned. I drew a blue square, red circle, yellow triangle, orange circle, green square, etc. When you finish drawing your colored shapes, explain to your toddler you will say a colored shape and your toddler will need to jump to the colored shaped you named. Continue this game as long as your toddler would like.

BONUS WEEK ACTIVITIES

WEDNESDAY

Easter Egg Matching

Materials
- ☐ Plastic Easter Eggs
- ☐ Cardboard Egg Carton
- ☐ Markers
- ☐ Bowl

Directions

To prepare this activity you will need colored markers that match the various colors of your plastic eggs. Now turn your egg carton upside down and use the markers to color the bottom of each egg compartment. You can color the compartments in random order. Lastly, separate the egg halves and place them in a bowl.

Ask your toddler if he would enjoy playing a color stacking game. Show him that he will pick an egg half from the bowl then find the matching color on the egg carton to place the egg half on. Your little one can stack eggs on top of each other. As your toddler is playing, ask him the color of the eggs he is picking up from the bowl. Your toddler can continue this game until the bowl is empty.

THURSDAY

Ice Cube Painting

Materials
- ☐ Ice Cube Tray
- ☐ Water
- ☐ Food Coloring
- ☐ Popsicle Sticks

Directions

You will need to prepare this activity overnight. To do so, fill your ice cube tray segments ¾ full of water. Next, add a few drops of different food coloring to each ice cube segment and stir. If you only have the four basic food colors (red, blue, yellow and green), then you can mix them together to make other colors. Mix red and yellow to make orange; mix blue and red together to make purple; and mix all the colors together to make black. Cut some popsicle sticks in half and place in the water. Place the ice cube tray in the freezer and let it sit overnight.

The next day, ask your toddler if he would enjoy painting with ice cube paintbrushes. Show your toddler the fun ice cube paintbrushes you created. Point to each ice cube and ask your toddler its color. Now allow your toddler to paint using the ice cube paintbrushes. We painted our sidewalk outside, but you can also allow your toddler to paint a piece of paper using the ice cube paintbrushes.

FRIDAY

Pin the Tail on the Bunny

Materials
- ☐ Bunny Activity Page (Appendix S)
- ☐ Scissors

Directions

Explain to your toddler that something silly happened and all of the bunnies lost their tails. Ask your toddler if he can help you find the correct tail for each bunny. Show him the *Bunny* activity page. You will need to cut out each bunny tail. Lay the bunny tails in front of your toddler. Ask him to pick up a tail. Ask your toddler the color of each bunny's tail. Ask him if he can place each tail on the matching bunny. Do this until all bunnies have a tail.

Appendix

To print the appendix, please visit:

www.bestmomideas.com/sendmycolorappendix

Password: bestmomideas9cx1

(Hint: I found it's easier to print the appendix pages than to copy or tear them from the bound book. ☺)

cut along line

APPENDIX A

Toddler Lesson Plans: Learning Colors | Autumn McKay

Appendix B

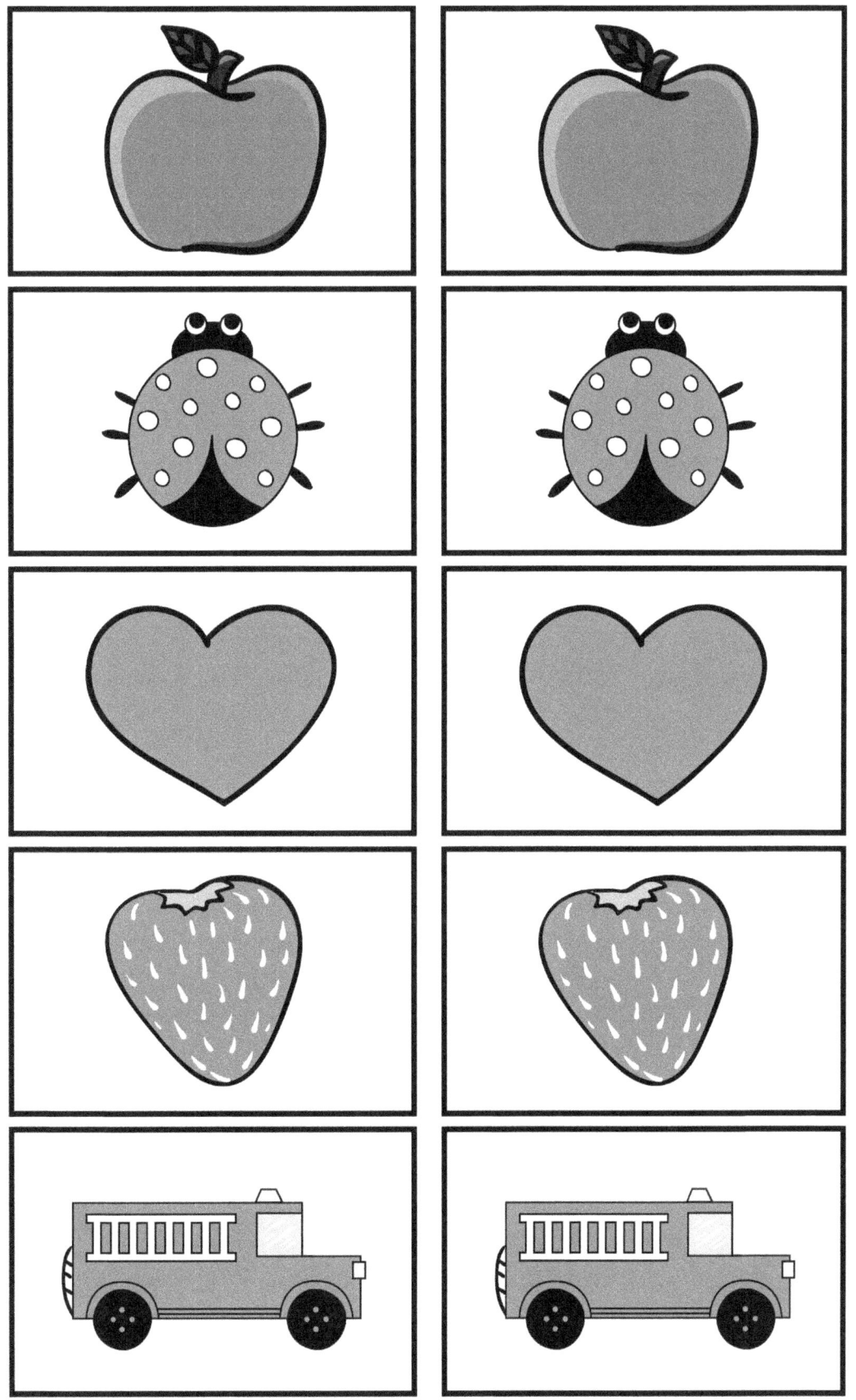

Toddler Lesson Plans: Learning Colors | Autumn McKay

Appendix C

Toddler Lesson Plans: Learning Colors | Autumn McKay

APPENDIX D

Toddler Lesson Plans: Learning Colors | Autumn McKay

cut along line

APPENDIX E

Toddler Lesson Plans: Learning Colors | Autumn McKay

APPENDIX F

Toddler Lesson Plans: Learning Colors | Autumn McKay

Appendix G

APPENDIX H

Toddler Lesson Plans: Learning Colors | Autumn McKay

Appendix 1

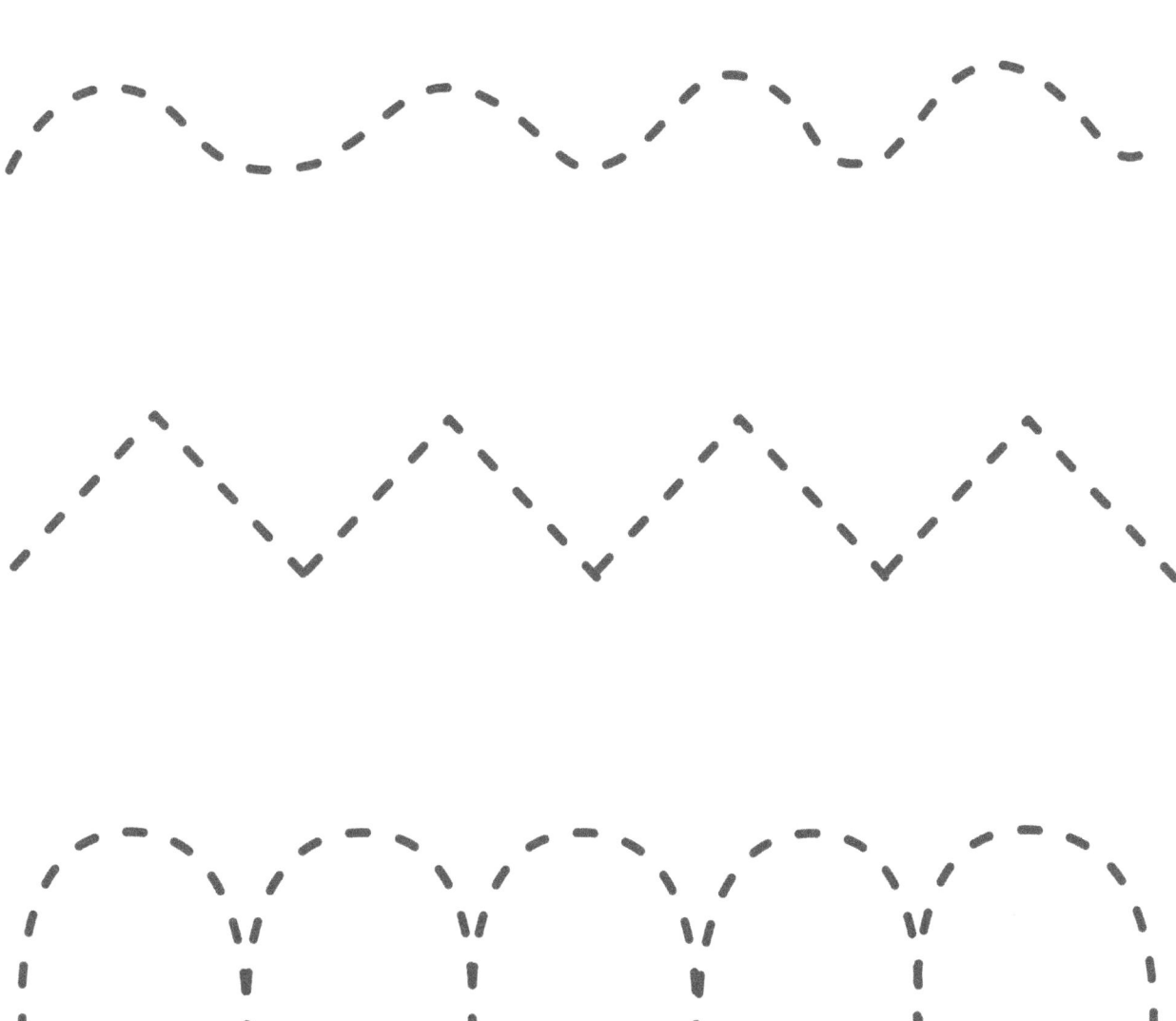

Toddler Lesson Plans: Learning Colors | Autumn McKay

APPENDIX J

Toddler Lesson Plans: Learning Colors | Autumn McKay

Appendix K

1 2 3 4 5

Toddler Lesson Plans: Learning Colors | Autumn McKay

Appendix L

Toddler Lesson Plans: Learning Colors | Autumn McKay

APPENDIX L (2)

Toddler Lesson Plans: Learning Colors | Autumn McKay

APPENDIX M

Toddler Lesson Plans: Learning Colors | Autumn McKay

APPENDIX N

Toddler Lesson Plans: Learning Colors | Autumn McKay

Appendix O

Toddler Lesson Plans: Learning Colors | Autumn McKay

APPENDIX P

Toddler Lesson Plans: Learning Colors | Autumn McKay

APPENDIX Q

Toddler Lesson Plans: Learning Colors | Autumn McKay

APPENDIX R

Toddler Lesson Plans: Learning Colors | Autumn McKay

APPENDIX S

Toddler Lesson Plans: Learning Colors | Autumn McKay

APPENDIX S (2)

cut along line

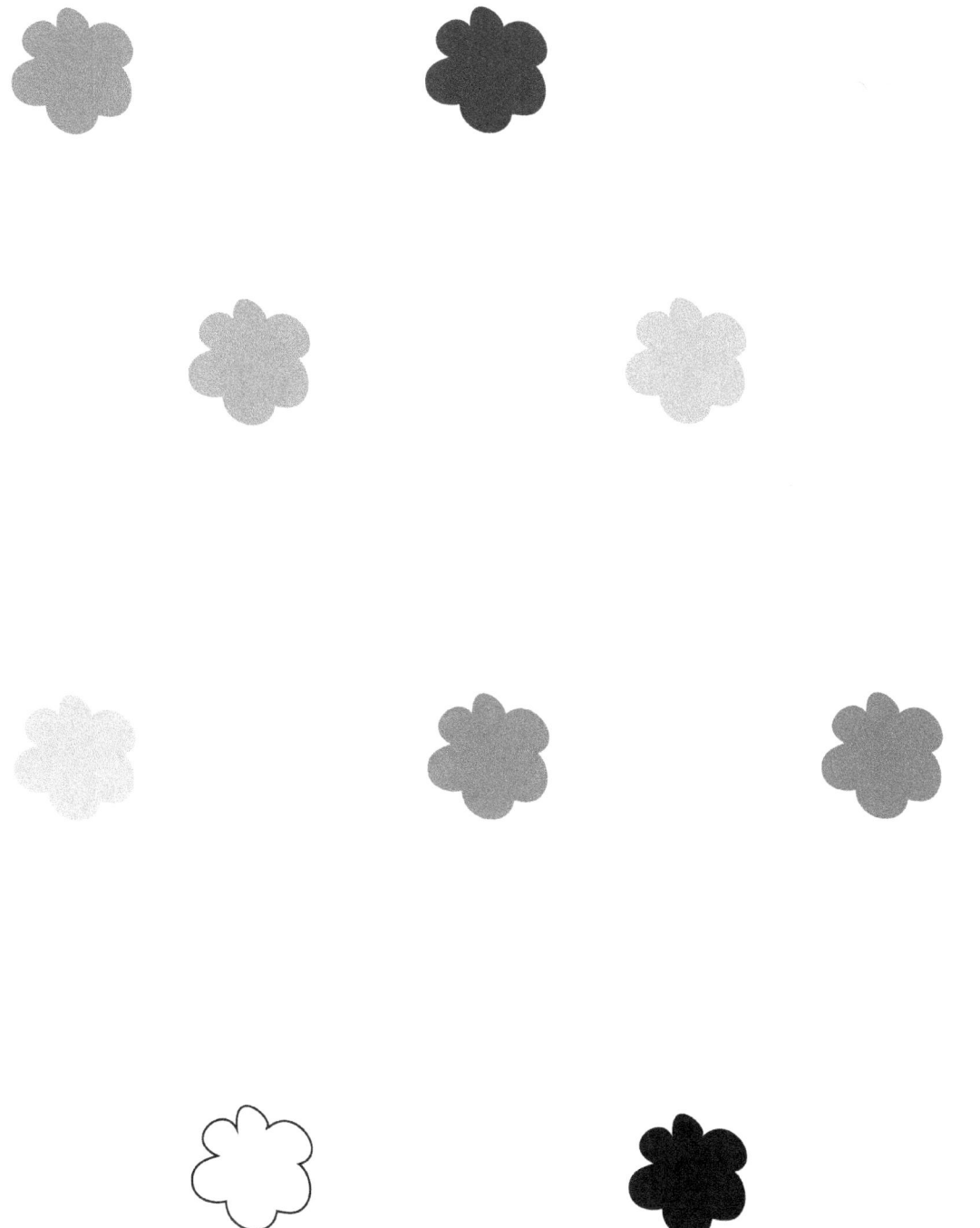

Toddler Lesson Plans: Learning Colors | Autumn McKay

Toddler Lesson Plans: LEARNING ABC'S

Twenty-six week guide to help your toddler learn ABC's and numbers

Written by Autumn McKay

PREVIEW

UNIT OVERVIEW

	Monday	Tuesday	Wednesday	Thursday	Friday	Alternate Activity
Letter A	Apple seed counting	Color uppercase and lowercase A's	Apple taste test	Make an A for alligator picture	Letter A mystery bag	Apple printing
Letter B	Outline a B with beans	Make a B for bunny picture	Bumblebee matching	Make homemade bread and butter	Letter B mystery bag	Blow bubbles
Letter C	Make a C for car picture	Read *If you Give a Cat a Cupcake* and make cupcakes	Park cars on the correct number	Sort coins into different bowls	Letter C mystery bag	Make clouds
Letter D	Dot shapes	Dig for dinosaurs	Make a D for duck picture	Feed the dogs	Letter D mystery bag	Visit a dog shelter
Letter E	Make elephant toothpaste	Make an E for elephant picture	Match Easter eggs	Place eggs in the nest	Letter E mystery bag	Make an elephant mask
Letter F	Make a fizzy balloon	Flower experiment	Five green frogs on a log	Make a F for fox picture	Letter F mystery bag	Paint with feathers
Letter G	Outline a G with grapes	Make a guitar	Make a G for goat picture	Make green goo	Letter G mystery bag	Gravity experiment
Letter H	Make an H for horse picture	Paint a hedgehog	Match helicopters	Find the heart number	Letter H mystery bag	Make hedgehog sandwiches
Letter I	Color a picture of an iguana	Make an I for insect picture	Make an igloo	Make insects in a jar	Letter I mystery bag	Make homemade ice cream in a bag
Letter J	Make a J for jellyfish picture	Play with jello	Make a jellyfish in a jar	Make jelly	Letter J mystery bag	Jumping J's
Letter K	Make a kite	Kick the ball	Make a K for kangaroo picture	Make a key	Letter K mystery bag	Kitten knitting
Letter L	Make an L for ladybug picture	Make lemonade	Make a lion mask	Make a lava lamp	Letter L mystery bag	Lace the letter L
Letter M	Magic Milk	Make an M for mouse picture	Sort M&M's	Read *If you Give a Moose a Muffin* and make muffins	Letter M mystery bag	Make maracas

UNIT OVERVIEW

	Monday	Tuesday	Wednesday	Thursday	Friday	Alternate Activity
Letter N	Make a necklace	Play in noodles	Make an N for night picture	Make rice krispy treat nests	Letter N mystery bag	Number activity
Letter O	Make an O for ostrich picture	Octopus math	Make waffle owls	O stamping	Letter O mystery bag	Otter puppet
Letter P	Make pizza	Make a P for penguin picture	Make Pom Pom shooters	Paint with popcorn	Letter P mystery bag	Find the letter on the pumpkin
Letter Q	Trace letters with a q-tip	Make quesadillas	Play in quicksand	Make a Q for quail picture	Letter Q mystery bag	Q-tip shapes
Letter R	Make straw rockets	Make an R for rooster picture	Robot size order	Rainbow matching	Letter R mystery bag	Make rain in a jar
Letter S	Make an S for snake picture	Paint squiggles	Star counting	Make s'mores	Letter S mystery bag	Shape puzzle
Letter T	Name train	Play tennis	Make a T for tree picture	Truck patterns	Letter T mystery bag	Make a turtle
Letter U	Utensil painting	Make a U for umbrella picture	Throw a balloon up	U toss	Letter U mystery bag	Learn positions, like under
Letter V	Make violins	Make a volcano	Make a V for vulture picture	Vegetable taste test	Letter V mystery bag	Vacuum the floor
Letter W	Make a windsock	Watermelon counting	Make a W for wagon picture	Make a whale snack	Letter W mystery bag	Make a walrus puppet
Letter X	X-ray hands	Make xylophone snack	X marks the spot patterns	Make an X for xylophone picture	Letter X mystery bag	Paper towel x-ray
Letter Y	Yarn maze	Make a Y for yak picture	Make a yo-yo	Make yogurt drops	Letter Y mystery bag	Wrap yarn around Y
Letter Z	Make a Z for zebra picture	Zip jackets	Zigzag race	Make a zebra mask	Letter Z mystery bag	Zebra tracks

Toddler Lesson Plans: Learning ABC's | Autumn McKay

ACTIVITY WEEK

MONDAY

Apple Seed Counting

Materials
- ☐ Apple counting activity page (Appendix A)
- ☐ Black beans

Directions

Explain to your toddler that apple starts with the letter A. You can also tell them the sound of the letter A. I like to tell my son the letter sound twice, and then say the word that starts with the letter, like "*a, a, apple.*" Then explain to your toddler that apples have seeds on the inside; you can even cut an apple in half to show them the seeds.

You will need the apple counting activity page. Show your toddler the numbers on the apples, and ask them to count with you as you point to the numbers on the apples. After you count together, tell your toddler that they will now be putting apple seeds on the apples. You will help your toddler place the correct number of apple seeds (black beans) on each apple. For example, your toddler will place one black bean on the number one apple. As you work through the activity together, ask them to tell you what apple starts with. You can also ask them what sound the letter A makes.

TUESDAY

Coloring Upper and Lowercase A's

Materials
- ☐ Upper and lowercase A activity page (Appendix B)
- ☐ Green crayon
- ☐ Red crayon

Directions

Show your toddler the upper and lowercase A activity page. Tell them that the letter A can be big and point to the uppercase A on the activity page, or the letter A can be little and point to the lowercase A of the activity page. Ask your little one what sound the letter A makes. Tell your toddler that airplane starts with the letter A. Tell them that they will color all of the big A's red.

You can chose different colors if you wish. Hand them the red crayon and ask them to find the big A's; you can assist as needed. Once all of the uppercase A's are colored, hand your toddler the green crayon and ask them to color the little a's green.

ACTIVITY WEEK

WEDNESDAY

Apple Taste Test

Materials
- ☐ 3 or 4 different types of apples
- ☐ Plate
- ☐ Knife

Directions
Use the knife to cut the apples into slices—this is an adult job. Place one slice of each apple on a plate. Sit down with your toddler, and ask them to tell you what letter apple starts with. See if they remember the sound that the letter A makes.

Tell them that they will taste different kinds of apples. Have them pick out which apple they want to try first. After they eat it, ask them if it was crunchy, sour, sweet, etc. Do this with each apple. After they try each apple, ask them which one was their favorite.

THURSDAY

Make an A for Alligator Picture

Materials
- ☐ Alligator activity page (Appendix C)
- ☐ Construction paper
- ☐ Scissors
- ☐ Glue
- ☐ Crayons

Directions
Let your toddler color each part of the alligator activity page. Then cut out the pieces from the alligator activity page. Ask your toddler to pick out a piece of construction paper to which to glue the alligator. Assemble the alligator, unglued, on the construction paper so that your little one can see what the finished product should look like. Tell your toddler that alligator starts with the letter A. Then tell them the sound, like "*a, a, alligator.*" Ask them to repeat it back to you.

Ask your toddler to help rub glue on each piece of the alligator, although you might have to assist if this is their first time using glue, and press the pieces onto the construction paper. After the alligator is complete, find a place to hang the picture so that your little one can be proud of their work.

# ACTIVITY WEEK

FRIDAY

Letter A Mystery Bag

Materials
- ☐ 4 objects that start with the letter A (ex. apple, airplane puzzle piece, acorn)
- ☐ 4 objects that start with a different letter (ex. book, key, lemon)
- ☐ Duffle Bag

Directions

Put all 8 objects in to the duffle bag. Tell your toddler that there are a lot of surprises in your bag. Explain that some surprises start with the letter A, and some surprises don't start with the letter A. Ask them to reach into your bag and pull out one surprise. Ask them what the object is that they pulled out. Say the name of the object together, and sound out the first letter of the object's name together. Ask your toddler if the object starts with A. If it does start with an A, then put it in one pile, but if it doesn't put it in a different pile.

For example, if your toddler pulls out a book. Ask them the name of the object. Then you would say "book" together. Sound out the first letter of book to your toddler, like *"b, b, book."* Then ask them if book starts with A. After they answer, put the book in the "doesn't start with A" pile.

ALTERNATE ACTIVITY

Apple Printing

Materials
- ☐ Paper
- ☐ 1 apple
- ☐ 2 colors of paint
- ☐ 2 paper plates
- ☐ Knife

Directions

First, you will need to cut the apple in half. You can cut it in half at the stem or along the middle. Put one half of the apple on each plate with each color of paint. Tell your toddler that they will be painting with apples. Ask your toddler to tell you what letter apple starts with, and then ask them what sound the letter A makes. They will dip the apple into the paint and then stamp it onto the paper.

After they are finished, let the painting dry, and then you can help them hang the painting in a special place.

Appendix A

Toddler Lesson Plans: Learning ABC's | Autumn McKay

Appendix B

Toddler Lesson Plans: Learning ABC's | Autumn McKay

APPENDIX C

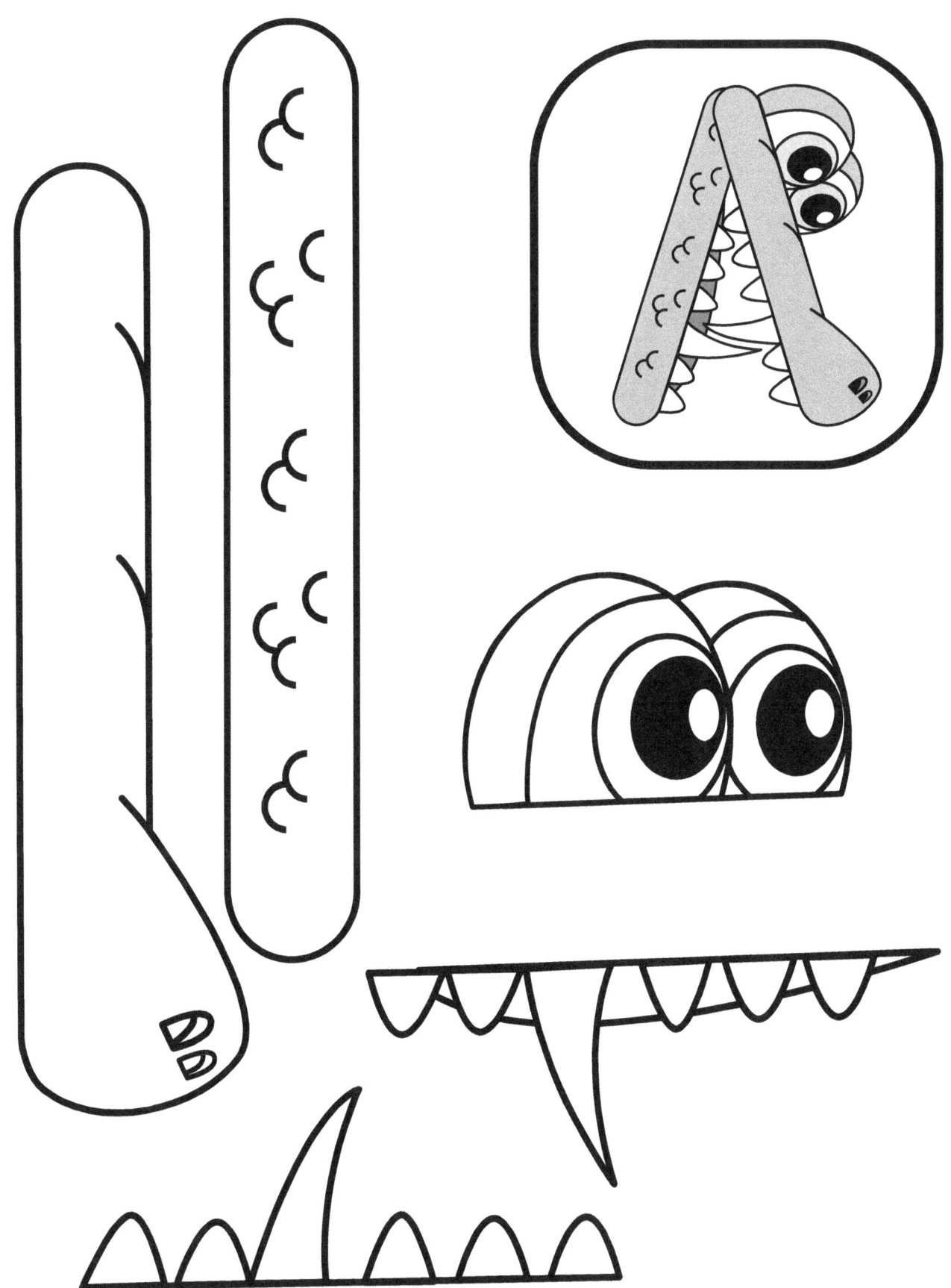

Toddler Lesson Plans: Learning ABC's | Autumn McKay

THE LITTLE ENGINEER

COLORING BOOK

NUMBERS

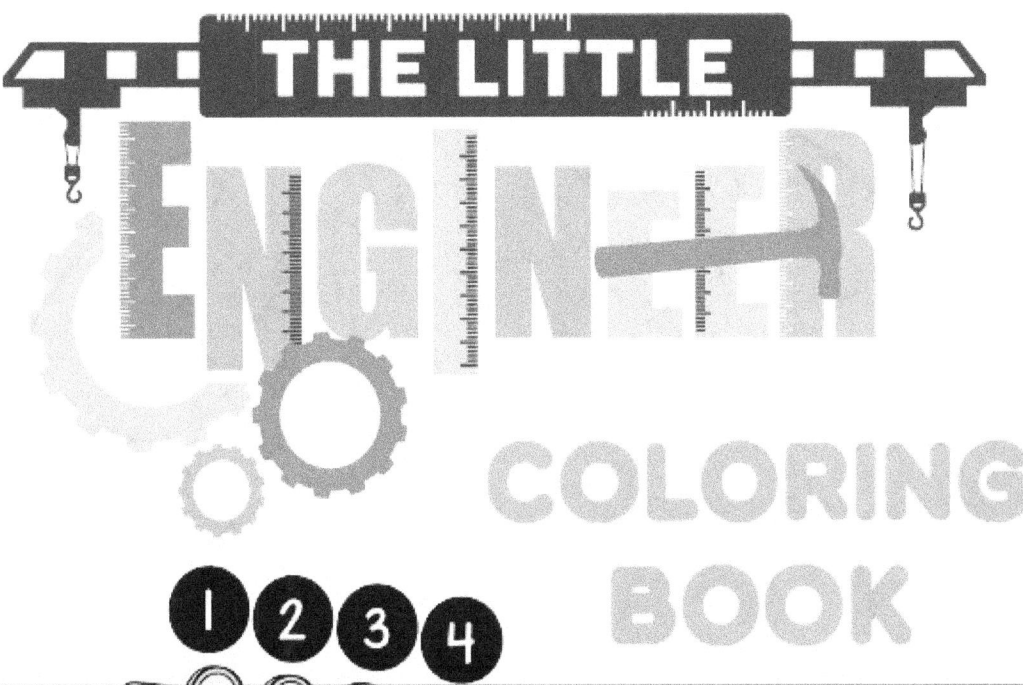

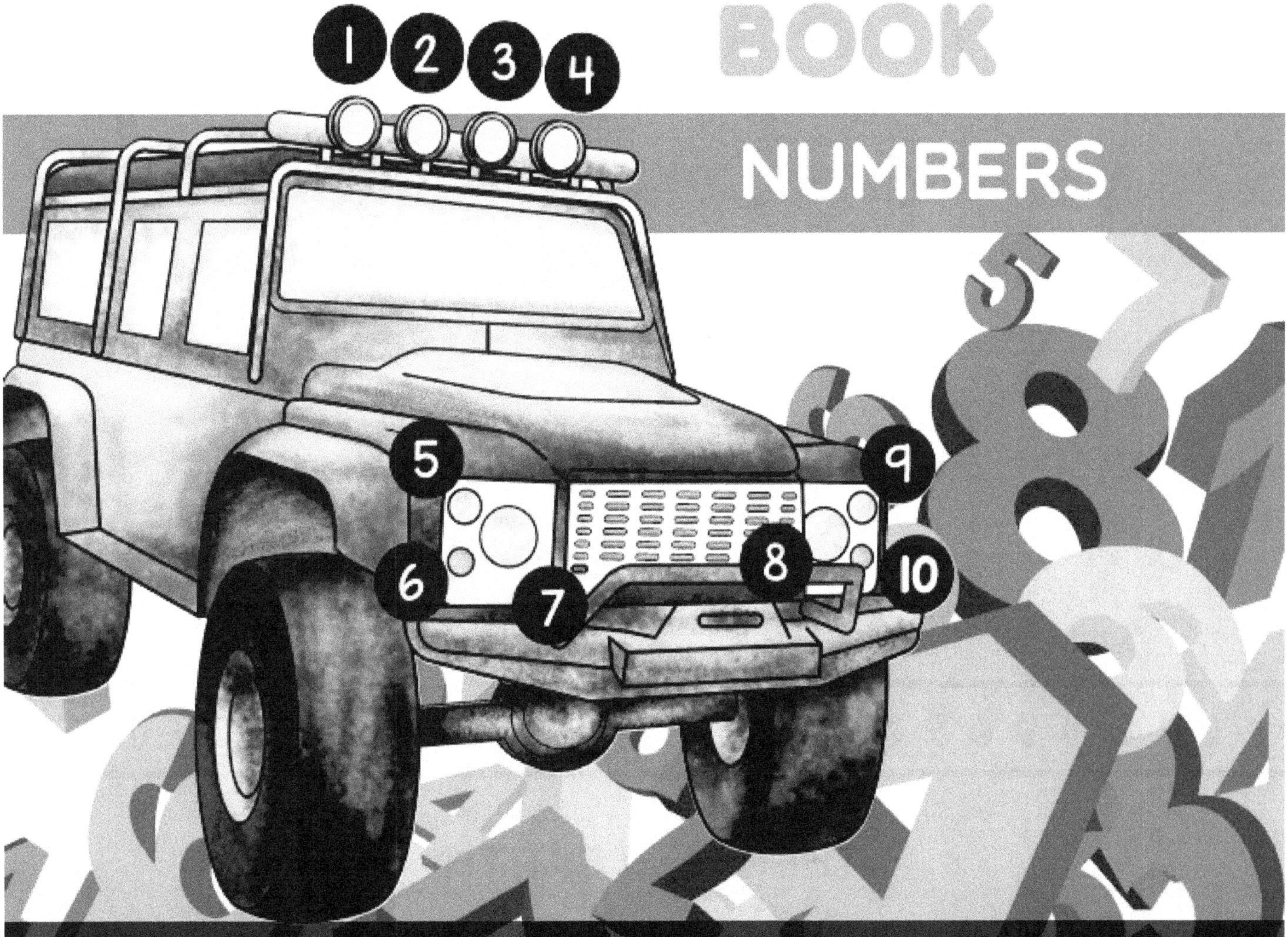

PREVIEW

0 1 2 3 4 5 6 7 8 9 10 11 12 13 14 15 16 17 18 19 20

THERE IS 1 EARTH.

EARTH IS THE PLANET WE LIVE ON, AND EARTH IS THE BEST PLACE TO LIVE IN OUR SOLAR SYSTEM.

2

◎ 1 2 3 4 5 6 7 8 9 10 11 12 13 14 15 16 17 18 19 20

A MOTORCYCLE HAS 2 WHEELS.

BICYCLES ALSO HAVE 2 WHEELS, BUT TRICYCLES HAVE 3 WHEELS.

3

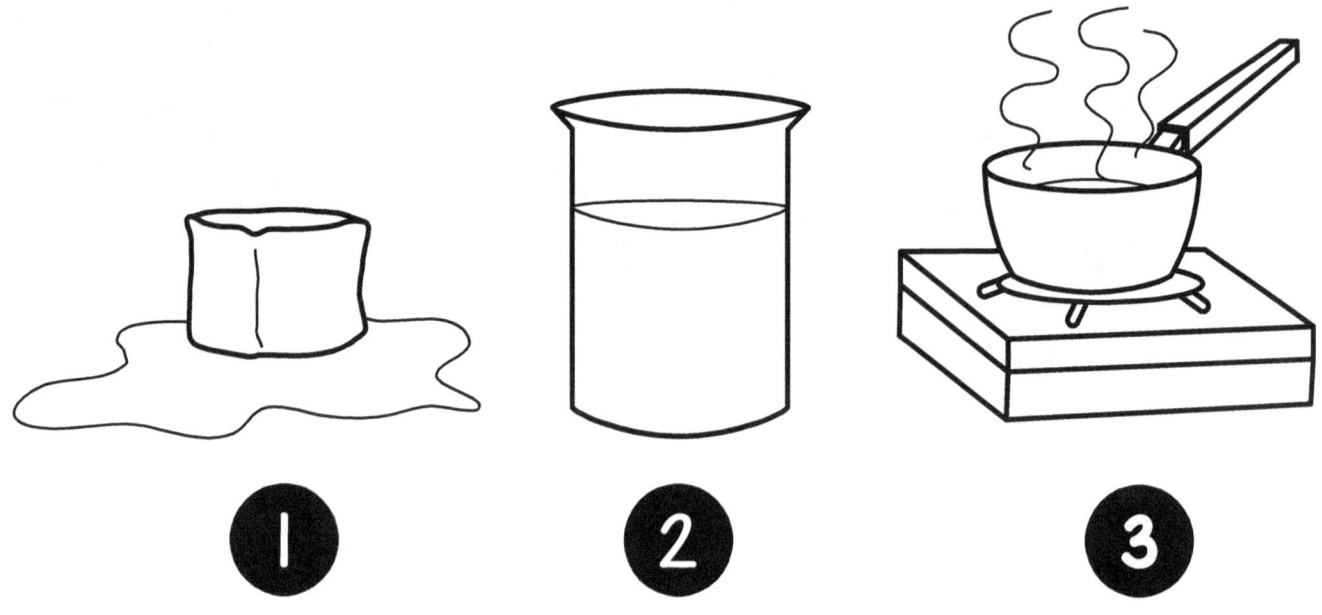

◎ 1 2 3 4 5 6 7 8 9 10 11 12 13 14 15 16 17 18 19 20

WATER CAN COME IN 3 FORMS.

WATER CAN BE SOLID (LIKE ICE CUBES), LIQUID (LIKE THE WATER WE DRINK) OR GAS (LIKE STEAM WHEN COOKING SPAGHETTI).

Thank you for welcoming me into your home!
I hope you and your child liked learning together with this book!

If you enjoyed this book, it would mean so much to me
if you wrote a review so other moms can learn from your experience.

Autumn@BestMomIdeas.com

Discover Autumn's Other Books

Early Learning Series

Early Learning Workbook Series

www.BestMomIdeas.com    @BestMomIdeas    Best Mom Ideas